INSECT WORLD
DIVING BEETLES

SANDRA MARKLE

UNDERWATER INSECT PREDATORS

⌐ LERNER PUBLICATIONS COMPANY MINNEAPOLIS

FOR CURIOUS KIDS EVERYWHERE

ACKNOWLEDGMENTS

The author would like to thank Dr. Robert Roughley, Department of Entomology, University of Manitoba, Canada, for sharing his expertise and enthusiasm. The author would also like to thank Dr. Simon Pollard, Curator of Invertebrate Zoology at Canterbury Museum, Christchurch, New Zealand, for his help with the scientific name pronunciation guides. Finally, a special thanks to Skip Jeffery, who shared the effort and joy of creating this book.

Lerner Publications Company
A division of Lerner Publishing Group, Inc.
241 First Avenue North
Minneapolis, MN 55401

Website address: www.lernerbooks.com

Library of Congress Cataloging-in-Publication Data

Markle, Sandra.
     Diving beetles : underwater insect predators / by Sandra Markle.
          p.   cm. — (Insect world)
     Includes bibliographical references and index.
     ISBN 978–0–8225–7295–4 (lib. bdg. : alk. paper)
       1. Dytiscidae—Juvenile literature. I. Title.
   QL596.D9M37 2008
   595.76'2—dc22   2007025243

Manufactured in the United States of American
1 2 3 4 5 6 – DP – 13 12 11 10 09 08

CONTENTS

WELCOME TO THE WORLD OF INSECTS—

those animals nicknamed bugs. It truly is the insects' world. Scientists have discovered more than a million kinds—more than any other kind of animal. And they are everywhere—even on the frozen continent of Antarctica.

So how can you tell if an animal is an insect rather than a relative like this tick *(shown below)*? Both belong to a group of animals called arthropods (AR-throh-podz). The animals in this group all share some traits. They have bodies divided into segments, jointed legs, and a stiff exoskeleton. This is a skeleton on the outside like a suit of armor. But one sure way to tell if an animal is an insect is to count its legs. All adult insects have six legs. They're the only animals in the world with six legs.

This book is about diving beetles, a kind of beetle that can be found in lakes, streams, and ponds throughout much of the world. Everywhere the diving beetle lives, it is a successful predator, hunting and eating prey to live.

BEETLE FACT

Like all insects, a diving beetle's body temperature rises and falls with the temperature around it. So it must warm up before it can hunt.

OUTSIDE AND INSIDE

ON THE OUTSIDE

Take a look at this adult female diving beetle. If you could touch it, its body would feel like tough plastic. That's because instead of having a hard, bony skeleton inside the way you do, an insect has an exoskeleton. This hard coat covers its whole body—even its eyes. The exoskeleton is made up of separate plates connected by stretchy tissue. This lets it bend and move. Check out the other key parts that all adult diving beetles share.

THORAX

HEAD

COMPOUND EYES:
What look like big eyes are really hundreds of eye units packed together. These let the insect look in every direction at once.

ANTENNA:
This is one of a pair of movable feelers. Hairs on the antennae detect chemicals for taste and smell.

MANDIBLES:
These are hard, toothlike jaws on the outside of the mouth. They are used to bite and grind.

Females have ridges on their elytra. Males don't.

OVIPOSITOR: The end of the female's abdomen. It is used for laying eggs.

WINGS: Diving beetles have two pairs of wings. A hard front pair, called the elytra, covers the hind pair. All wings are attached to the thorax.

ABDOMEN

SPIRACLES: These holes down the sides of the thorax and abdomen let air into and out of the body for breathing.

LEGS AND FEET: These are used for walking, swimming, and holding on. All legs are attached to the thorax.

ON THE INSIDE

Now, look inside an adult female diving beetle.

HEART:
This muscular tube pumps blood toward the head. Then the blood flows throughout the body.

BRAIN: This receives messages from the antennae, eyes, and sensory hairs. It sends signals to control all body parts.

ESOPHAGUS:
Food passes through this tube between the mouth and the crop.

CROP:
The crop holds food before it moves on for further digestion.

Approved by Dr. Robert Roughley, University of Manitoba

RECTUM:
Wastes collect here and
pass out an opening
called the anus.

INTESTINE (GUT):
Digestion is completed
here. Food nutrients
pass into the body cavity
to enter the blood
and flow to all
body parts.

SPERMATHECA:
This sac stores
sperm after
mating.

MALPIGHIAN
TUBULES: These
clean the blood and
pass wastes to the
intestine.

OVARY:
This body
part produces
eggs.

NERVE CORD:
This is the insect's
nervous system. It
sends messages between
the brain and other
body parts.

BECOMING AN ADULT

Insect babies grow into adults in two ways: complete metamorphosis (me-teh-MOR-feh-sus) and incomplete metamorphosis. Metamorphosis means change. Diving beetles go through complete metamorphosis. Their life includes four stages: egg, larva, pupa, and adult. Each stage looks and behaves very differently.

IN INCOMPLETE METAMORPHOSIS, insects go through three stages: egg, nymph, and adult. Nymphs are much like small adults. But nymphs can't reproduce.

LARVA

PUPA

The focus of a diving beetle's life is hunting. Diving beetle larvae are predators. So are the adults. Both hunt underwater for prey such as other insects, fish, and tadpoles. But diving beetle larvae look very different from the adults. The way they hunt is very different too. Diving beetle larvae are built to hide and ambush prey. Adult diving beetles are built to chase down prey. Every environment has its chain of hunters. In slow-moving water habitats, diving beetle larvae and adults are successful predators.

BEETLE FACT

Diving beetle larvae are such fierce hunters that they are sometimes called water tigers.

ADULT

ADULTS GO HUNTING

An adult diving beetle watches for prey with two big compound eyes. Each of your eyes has a single lens and layer of light-sensitive cells. But a beetle's big compound eyes are hundreds of separate eye units. These are aimed up, down, forward, and to the sides. The diving beetle can look in all directions at once. These eye units probably do not see as sharply as your eyes do. But having lots of eyes watching lets the diving beetle quickly notice something moving. Compound eyes help the beetle stay alert for predators, like fish and birds, as it looks for its own prey.

BEETLE FACT

Many kinds of adult insects also have simple eyes, eyes that sense light from dark. Diving beetles do not. Diving beetle larvae, though, only have simple eyes.

A BREATH AWAY

An adult diving beetle needs to breathe oxygen from the air. Still, it is able to stay underwater long enough to hunt and catch prey. That's because it carries a supply of air with it. When the beetle is near the surface, it pokes its rear end out of the water. Then when it dives, air is trapped between the shell-like elytra, or front wings, and the insect's abdomen. This bubble of air is held in place over the diving beetle's spiracles by the elytra. The spiracles are the openings that let air into and out of the beetle's body when it breathes. The air bubble acts like a scuba diver's air tank.

BEETLE FACT

Adult diving beetles can stay underwater as long as 10 to 15 minutes.

THE CHASE

To launch its attack, the adult diving beetle kicks its big hind legs. It paddles with both hind legs at once as though rowing a boat. Besides being strong, the beetle's hind legs are fringed with hairs. Those hairs spread out on each backward, power stroke. This makes the beetle's hind legs even bigger, more powerful paddles. When the beetle pulls its legs forward again, those hairs fold up. This lets the water flow past easily without slowing the beetle down.

BEETLE FACT

Adult diving beetles have been timed kicking as fast as twice a second!

The adult diving beetle's body is shaped to slice easily through the water. The hard elytra help reduce drag. Drag is when water around an object slows it down. A smooth wax coating on the diving beetle's exoskeleton also helps the beetle zip through the water in hot pursuit of prey.

Even if the prey twists and turns, the beetle stays on its trail. The beetle's antennae have tiny hairs that sense changes in water currents. In murky or muddy water, the hunter's antennae help it keep track of its prey.

BEETLE FACT

If caught by a predator, such as a fish, the diving beetle gives off a chemical. This must taste bad. The diving beetle is usually quickly set free.

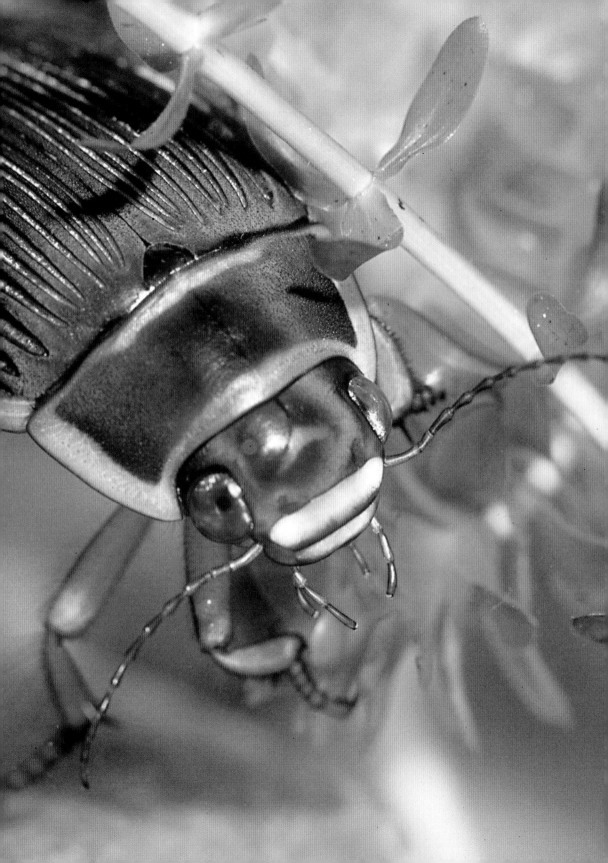

MAKING THE KILL

Kicking hard, the adult diving beetle closes in on its meal. Then it reaches out its front and middle legs and grabs it. Chemical sensors around its mouth let it "taste" its catch. This way, the hunter makes sure that what it has caught is food. If the prey passes this test, the diving beetle takes a bite. Then it bites again. In this way, the diving beetle kills its prey by eating it, bit by bit.

LARVAE HUNT TOO

A diving beetle larva does not go in search of prey. Instead, it slips in among underwater plants. There the larva's slender body and dull coloring help it to blend in. It stays perfectly still, waiting for little fish or insects to swim close. Like the adult diving beetle, the larva needs oxygen from the air. It has just one opening for breathing. This opening is at the tail end of its abdomen. Like a swimmer with a snorkel, the larva pokes its rear end out of the water. It breathes through its tail opening while it stays hidden and waits.

BEETLE FACT

There is a fringe of hair around the larva's rear end. This keeps water's natural film, called surface tension, from sealing the breathing opening.

TAKING A BITE

Diving beetle larvae have only simple eyes. Their eyes are able to sense light from dark. They can't see well enough to chase after prey. But their eyes see enough to warn larvae something is coming close. Then they can strike if it is prey or hide from anything bigger. Their weapons are their big jaws.

These jaws are sharp and hollow. The larva sinks them into its prey. Then it pumps digestive juices through them. The juices dissolve the prey's insides the way your spit softens a cracker in your mouth. And when the insides are soft as soup, the larva sucks in its meal.

GROWING UP HUNTING

Like the adult, the diving beetle larva has an exoskeleton.
Soon the larva grows so much that its exoskeleton becomes
tight. Then it molts, or sheds, its armorlike covering. There is
already a new coat underneath. This new coat is soft at first.
The larva waits for the coat to harden before it starts hunting
again. Because the larva is bigger, it's able to catch bigger
prey. The larva gets the energy it needs to grow bigger again.
After about six weeks of growing and molting, the diving
beetle larva crawls out of the pond and digs into the mud.

Next, the larva goes through its pupa stage. It seems to be resting. Inside the pupa, a lot of activity is going on, though. The larval body parts are breaking down. The adult parts are forming. About two weeks later, the pupa splits open. An adult crawls out and heads back to the pond.

BEETLE FACT

A diving beetle larva usually molts three times.

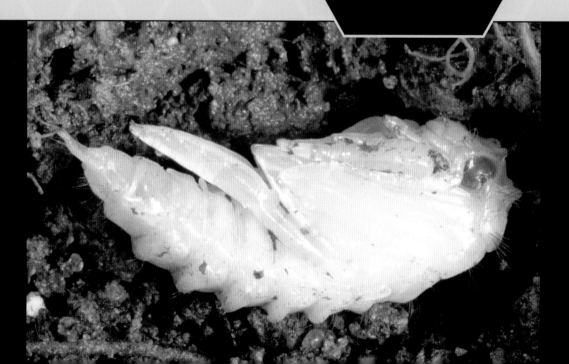

A HUNTING TRIP

It is now autumn. The weather is hot and dry, and the pond is drying up. This male diving beetle can only find a worm to eat. Luckily, as an adult, he does not have to stay where the hunting is poor. He has wings, so he can fly away to find a better hunting site. That night, he crawls up a twig and out of the water. He spreads his wings for the first time.

BEETLE FACT

Before flying, a diving beetle shivers to warm up its flight muscles.

The diving beetle's hard, curved elytra are shaped like an airplane's wings. They catch a breeze to help him lift off. Then he flaps his back wings hard to fly. He flies until he sees a bright glow. It's the surface of a pond reflecting moonlight. The male diving beetle senses this is a place to go hunting. So he closes his wings, clamps his legs against his body, and dives in. He quickly spots a little fish and catches a meal. If he finds enough prey to eat, he'll stay. If not, he'll fly off again and search for a better hunting site.

BEETLE FACT

Diving beetles prefer to live in standing or slow-flowing water. They like it best if there are lots of plants.

SLEEPING THROUGH HARD TIMES

Sometimes, no place has enough prey. In the warm places, there is usually poor hunting in the dry season. Farther north, diving beetles have trouble finding prey during the winter when the weather is cold.

This male diving beetle lives in the northern United States. So when the weather turns cold, he dives to the pond bottom. He digs in and hibernates, or goes into a kind of sleep. His body slows down in this resting state, and he needs very little oxygen. He can stay underwater all winter long.

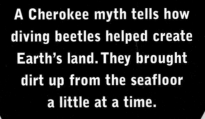

BEETLE FACT

A Cherokee myth tells how diving beetles helped create Earth's land. They brought dirt up from the seafloor a little at a time.

FINDING A MATE

Finally, spring comes again. The weather warms up, and so does the pond. The male diving beetle swims to the surface to breathe. Then he starts hunting again. Before long, he's ready to mate. He again takes flight. His antennae help him track a female diving beetle. Females usually don't fly to find a mate. Instead, they climb up a plant stem and give off pheromones. These are special scents that attract males.

The female diving beetle is a little larger than the male. She needs to be bigger. She has to catch bigger prey to get enough food energy to produce eggs. She also needs to be bigger for her abdomen to hold all the eggs she makes.

BEETLE FACT

Males have parts on their front legs that work like suction cups. They use these to hold onto the female during mating.

MALE

FEMALE

LAYING EGGS

The male dies not long after mating. The female keeps on hunting for a few more weeks. Then she climbs up the stem of a water plant. She uses her ovipositor, her sharp tail end, to cut a slit into the stem. She lays one egg in this slit. She makes another slit in a stem and lays another egg. She does this over and over until she lays nearly a hundred eggs in all. Not long after she finishes laying her eggs, the female diving beetle dies too.

BEETLE FACT

Diving beetles produce lots of young. That way, some will survive to grow up.

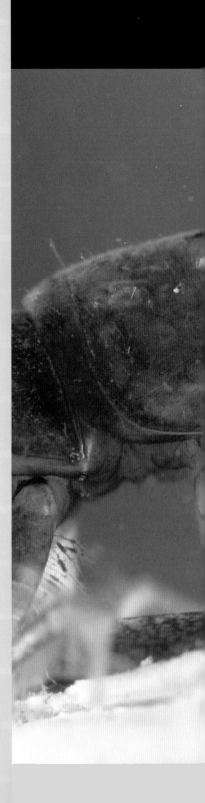

BORN TO HUNT

Just three to four days after an egg is laid, the diving beetle larva hatches. It drops into the water below. There, it swims among the plants. Many diving beetle larvae are eaten by fish and birds. But this larva stays safe. It pokes the tip of its snorkel-like rear end into the air while it waits. Suddenly, it senses a newt swimming by. It strikes, sinking in its big jaws. One of a new generation of diving beetles has become a successful predator.

DIVING BEETLES AND OTHER INSECT PREDATORS

DIVING BEETLES belong to a group, or order, of insects called Coleoptera (KOH-lee-ap-tuh-ruh). That name comes from the Greek words for sheath and wings. It was given this name because of its hard front wings, or elytra. There are more than 350,000 different kinds of beetles. There are more than 5,000 different kinds of diving beetles worldwide. This makes them the largest group in the insect class.

SCIENTISTS GROUP living and extinct animals with others that are similar. So beetles are classified this way:

    Kingdom: Animalia
    Phylum: Arthropoda
    Class: Insecta
    Order: Coleoptera

HELPFUL OR HARMFUL? Diving beetles are helpful because they eat mosquito larvae. Mosquitoes spread diseases that make people and animals sick. Diving beetles are also food for some animals, such as birds and larger fish.

HOW BIG ARE diving beetles? They can be up to 1.5 inches (3.8 centimeters) long.

MORE INSECT PREDATORS

Other insects also hunt for prey in order to live and reproduce. Compare these insect hunters to diving beetles.

Dragonflies are the world's fastest flying insects. The adults catch other flying insects in the air. They have huge eyes to spot fast-flying prey. Dragonflies go through complete metamorphosis but skip the pupa stage. The larvae are predators too. Most dragonfly larvae hunt underwater. They have a lower jaw that they can shoot out to hook prey, such as other insects, tadpoles, and little fish. Some kinds of dragonflies spend years as larvae. To become an adult, a larva crawls up a plant stem and out of the water. Then its exoskeleton splits open. The winged adult crawls out and flies away.

Robber flies often perch to watch for prey. The adults catch flying wasps, grasshoppers, and flies. They use their mouthparts to inject their saliva into their prey. This rapidly digests the prey's insides. Then the fly sucks in a liquid meal. Robber flies go through complete metamorphosis. The larvae are long and legless. They live in the soil. There they crawl to hunt and catch other insect larvae and worms.

Tiger beetle adults have long, slender legs and can run superfast. When they spot other insects, they chase them down and catch them with their big, sickle-shaped mandibles. Tiger beetle larvae are predators too. After hatching, the larva digs into the soil to build a burrow. From there, it ambushes any insect that comes close. Then it drags its prey into its burrow to eat it.

GLOSSARY

abdomen: the tail end of an insect. It contains the parts for digestion and reproduction.

adult: the final stage of an insect's life cycle

antennae: movable, jointed parts on the insect's head used for sensing

brain: receives messages from the antennae, eyes, and sensory hairs. It sends signals to control all body parts.

complete metamorphosis: a process of development in which the young looks and behaves very differently from the adult. Stages include egg, larva, pupa, and adult.

compound eyes: eyes that are really hundreds of eye units packed together. These let the insect look in every direction at once.

crop: area of the digestive system where food is held before it is passed on for further digestion

egg: a female reproductive cell; also the name given to the first stage of an insect's life cycle

elytra (EL-eh-truh)**:** hard, shell-like front wings of beetles

esophagus (ee-SAH-feh-gus)**:** a tube through which food passes from the mouth to the crop, or stomach

exoskeleton: protective, skeleton-like covering on the outside of the body

head: the insect's body part that has the mouth, the brain, and the sensory organs, such as the eyes and the antennae, if there are any

hibernate: when an insect's body slows down so much it can survive on stored food energy

incomplete metamorphosis: a process of development in which the young look and behave much like a small adult except that they are unable to reproduce. Stages include egg, nymph, and adult.

intestine (gut)**:** digestion is completed here. Food nutrients pass into the body cavity to enter the blood and flow to all body parts.

larva: the stage between egg and pupa in complete metamorphosis

Malpighian (mal-PEE-gee-an) **tubules:** the organ that cleans the blood and passes wastes to the intestine

mandibles: the grinding mouthparts of an insect

molt: the process of an insect shedding its exoskeleton

nerve cord: the nervous system. It sends messages between the brain and other body parts.

nymph: stage between egg and adult in incomplete metamorphosis

ovary (OH-vuh-ree)**:** body part that produces eggs

ovipositor: tail end of the abdomen used to deposit eggs and make an egg case

pheromones: chemical scents given off as a form of communication

predator: an animal that is a hunter

prey: an animal that a predator catches to eat

pupa: stage between larva and adult in complete metamorphosis. At this stage, the larva's body structure and systems are completely changed into its adult form.

rectum: part of the digestive system where wastes collect before passing out of the body

simple eyes: eyes only able to sense light from dark. These are the only kind of eyes diving beetle larvae have. Adult diving beetles have only compound eyes.

sperm: male reproductive cell

spermatheca (spur-muh-THEE-kuh)**:** sac in female insects that stores sperm after mating

spiracles (SPIR-i-kehlz)**:** holes down the sides of the thorax and abdomen. They let air into and out of the body for breathing.

thorax: the body part between the head and the abdomen

DIGGING DEEPER

To keep on investigating diving beetles and other kinds of beetles, explore these books and online sites.

BOOKS

Llewelly, Claire. *Beetles.* New York: Franklin Watts, 2002.
 Find out how to catch and keep beetles so you can watch them in action. Then, of course, you'll want to return them to their home environment.

McEvey, Shane F. *Beetles.* New York: Chelsea House Publications, 2001.
 Take a close look at a number of kinds of amazing beetles.

Pledger, Maurice. *All about Bugs and Beetles.* San Diego: Silver Dolphin Books, 2007.
 Discover amazing facts about bugs and beetles. Get close-up looks. Enjoy the extras: puzzles, stickers, learn-to-draw games, and more.

WEBSITES

Bug Facts: Giant Diving Beetle and Water Tiger

http://www.royalalbertamuseum.ca/natural/insects/bugsfaq/diving.htm

> Find out more about a giant diving beetle's life, habits, and habitat.

San Diego Zoo's Animal Bytes: Beetle

http://www.sandiegozoo.org/animalbytes/t-beetle.html

> Visit the zoo online and go beetle crazy. Don't miss the Photo
> Bytes for close-up looks at beetles.

The Sunburst Diving Beetle

http://www.insecthobbyist.com/articles/InsectHobbyist/DivingBeetle
.html

> Learn about the sunburst beetle, one kind of diving beetle.

DIVING BEETLE ACTIVITIES

ADOPT A POND

Diving beetles are part of a big family. Worldwide, there are more than 5,000 different kinds of diving beetles. Wherever you live, you are likely to find these water predators in clean freshwater. Diving beetle larvae are likely to die if their pond or stream gets polluted. The adults will fly away. Scientists often look for diving beetles when checking water quality.

If you live near a pond, look to see if diving beetles are there. You'll need a fine mesh dip net, such as an aquarium net or even a kitchen strainer. You'll also need a bucket and an adult partner. Have your partner skim the pond's surface with the net. Then have your partner dump the net into the bucket. Look at what was collected. Use the pictures in this book to check if you caught any diving beetles. Were there both larvae and adults? Return the animals to their water home. Then take samples at several other places around the edge of the pond. Did you find any diving beetles? Did you find a lot or only a few?

Think about how you might help protect the pond. Find out what your community is doing to keep the pond and other water environments healthy.

TRAP AIR THE WAY A DIVING BEETLE DOES

Adult diving beetles need to breathe air. When they dive to hunt underwater, they have to take air along with them. Try this to see how they use their elytra to trap air. First, fill a sink or a large container like a fish tank with water. Then hold a glass, open end down, above the water. Push the glass straight down into the water. While the glass is underwater, tip it to one side. You'll see bubbles roll out. The bubbles are formed by the air that was trapped inside the glass. The diving beetle sticks its rear end into the air and then dives underwater. Air is trapped between the insect's abdomen and hard, shell-like front wings like air in the glass. Oxygen from the trapped air moves into the diving beetle's body through its spiracles, the openings in its abdomen.

INDEX

PHOTO ACKNOWLEDGMENTS

The images in this book are used with the permission of: © Dwight R. Kuhn, p. 4; © Fabio Liverani/npl/Minden Pictures, p. 5; © Warren Photographic, pp. 6–7, 12–13; © Bill Hauser/Independent Picture Service, pp. 8–9; © Jane Burton/naturepl.com, p. 10 (left); © Bartomeu Borrell/Bruce Coleman, Inc., p. 10 (right); © William Kolvoort/naturepl.com, p. 11; © Geoff Dore/naturepl.com, p. 15; © Colin Milkins/Oxford Scientific Films/Photolibrary, p. 17; © Gerard Visser, www.microcosmos.nl, p. 19; © DAVID M. DENNIS/Animals Animals, p. 21; © Robert Pickett/CORBIS, p. 23; © Solvin Zankl/naturepl.com, pp. 24, 38–39; © Jason Smalley/naturepl.com, p. 25; © B. Borrell Casals; Frank Lane Picture Agency/CORBIS, p. 26; © Oxford Scientific Films/Photolibrary, pp. 27, 31, 37; © Stephen Dalton/Minden Pictures, pp. 29, 35, 41 (bottom); © Jim Hallett/Oxford Scientific Films/Photolibrary, p. 33; © Meul/ARCO/naturepl.com, p. 41 (top); © CISCA CASTELIJNS/FOTO NATURA/Minden Pictures, p. 41 (middle).

Front Cover: © Jane Burton/naturepl.com.